AF585391

AUSTRALIA'S REMARKABLE WILDLIFE

# DINGO

JOHN LESLEY

REDBACK publishing

First Published 2022 by
Redback Publishing
PO Box 357 Frenchs Forest NSW 2086
Australia

www.redbackpublishing.com
orders@redbackpublishing.com



ISBN 978-1-925860-96-2



Author: John Lesley
Editor: Caroline thomas
Design: Redback Publishing

NATIONAL LIBRARY OF AUSTRALIA
A catalogue record for this book is available from the National Library of Australia


Originated by Redback Publishing

Printed and bound in Malaysia

Acknowledgements
Abbreviations: l—left, r—right, b—bottom, t—top, c—centre, m—middle
We would like to thank the following for permission to reproduce photographs: (Images © shutterstock) Cover tr Maurizio De Mattei, p8bm Nicole Patience, p22cr Moshe EINHORN, p25br Annalucia.

# CONTENTS

# DINGO BASIC FACTS

## SCIENTIFIC NAME
*Canis lupus dingo*

## TYPE OF ANIMAL
Placental mammal

## SIZE
As big as a medium-sized dog

## COLOUR

Light to dark brown, often with white paws, snout, chest and tail tip.

## CONSERVATION STATUS

Dingoes were once widely hunted because of their habit of killing livestock. Protection varies across Australia. In some areas, dingoes are a protected native animal, while elsewhere they are considered pest animals and can be killed.

# ARE DINGOES DOGS?

Dingoes look like domestic dogs, but they are not domesticated. Because they are very intelligent, dingoes can be tamed and sometimes live the life of a pet, but they remain a wild animal.

Domestic animals, such as pet dogs, have evolved over thousands of years to be mostly trustworthy and fearless living with people. A domestic dog will seek out the company of people and sees them as part of its pack. Human company is not the first choice for a pure-bred dingo.

# WHERE DID DINGOES COME FROM?

The dingo is related to wolves that live in parts of Asia. How and when it managed to get to Australia is a mystery, but by about 4,000 years ago the dingo was well established on the Australian mainland.

Dingoes may have arrived with sailors from Asia, many of whom visited northern Australia and traded with the local Indigenous people over thousands of years.

# TYPES OF DINGOES

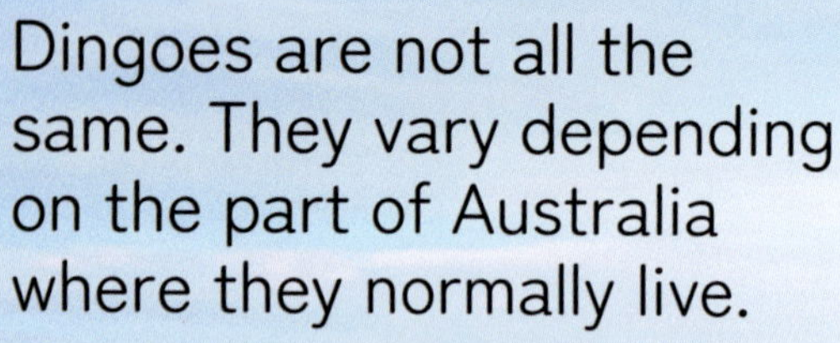

Dingoes are not all the same. They vary depending on the part of Australia where they normally live.

## ALPINE DINGOES

In Australia's high alps, the alpine dingo has evolved to have thicker fur to keep it warm in the cold winters.

Alpine dingo

Desert dingo

## DESERT DINGOES

In Australia's desert regions, dingoes have short, sandy-coloured fur. They have a naturally thin appearance, which causes many tourists to think they must be starving. This is not usually the case and trying to feed them is a very bad idea. Dingoes do not need help finding food in the wild, as they have been doing this successfully for millennia.

# WHERE DO DINGOES LIVE?

Dingoes live in a variety of habitats across all of Australia, except for Tasmania. They are found in alpine environments, in cold, snowy surroundings, in rainforests and in semi-arid and desert regions.

# DINGO LIFE CYCLE

The dingo is one of the few placental mammals that are native to Australia. The dingo puppy grows inside its mother and feeds on milk after birth.

A female dingo can produce up to six puppies in a litter. She finds a safe place to give birth, inside a cave, a burrow or a hollow log.

Dingoes live for about ten years in the wild, but longer in zoos where keepers can look after their health.

Dingo cross Smithfield herder

Dingoes and domestic dogs can breed together to produce cross-bred puppies.

# ARE DINGOES DANGEROUS?

Dingoes are dangerous animals. Their intelligence enables them to learn how to approach humans to get food, but they have also been responsible for attacking babies, children, pets and even adult humans.

Never feed wild dingoes. This encourages them to come too close to people and to lose their natural fear.

# FRASER ISLAND

There is a large population of dingoes on Fraser Island, off the coast of Queensland. After years of being fed by tourists, the dingoes have lost much of their fear and attacks on people have occurred.

Because of their isolation, the Fraser Island dingoes are probably the most pure-bred group in Australia.

# DINGOES AND FARMERS

Dingoes see lambs and calves as natural prey. To stop the spread of dingoes and wild dogs into farming country in the south of Australia, the Dingo Fence (or Dog Fence) was built in the 1880s, and has been mended many times since then. It runs across South Australia, New South Wales and Queensland, and its purpose is to stop or at least slow the spread of dingoes.

Today, dingoes, wild dogs and feral dogs are still a threat to livestock, even with the Dingo Fence in place. Farmers also rely on leaving poison baits on their properties to try to control the spread of dingoes and feral dogs.

# BLUE HEELER

The Australian cattle dog, also called a blue heeler, is today a separate breed. It is famous with farmers worldwide as a working dog.

The blue heeler's reputation as a loyal and hard worker contrasts sharply with the view farmers have of its dingo ancestors.

In the early 1800s, Thomas Hall in New South Wales crossed a dingo with his own dog. After further cross-breeding, the Australian cattle dog was eventually produced.

With a coat colour that can be red or grey-blue, the Australian cattle dog is one of Australia's most loved dog breeds.

# DINGO BEHAVIOUR

Dingoes rarely bark. They will howl and make other noises to communicate with each other.

Dingoes have territories which they defend against other dingoes. They mark their territory using smell by rubbing against things, urinating and defecating.

There is no equality in a dingo pack. The pack members with the lowest status are not allowed to breed, and they may also be stopped from eating when the pack kills an animal for food.

# HUNTING FOR FOOD

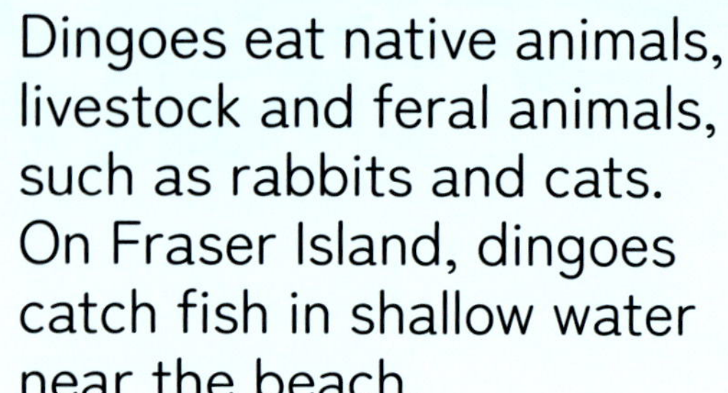

Dingoes eat native animals, livestock and feral animals, such as rabbits and cats. On Fraser Island, dingoes catch fish in shallow water near the beach.

Dingoes have learned that campers leave food in their tents and in rubbish dumps. They will come very close in an attempt to take food. Campers often report that dingoes have boldly entered their tent or taken food from a campsite.

Dingoes are the largest native, land-based carnivores in Australia. They may become prey to crocodiles, and dingo puppies can be taken by birds-of-prey, feral dogs or wild pigs.

# DINGOES AS PETS

Since wild dingoes look similar to dogs, many people would like to have a dingo as a pet.

Even when it is raised from birth as a pet, a dingo always remains a wild animal which has been tamed, not domesticated.

In some parts of Australia, dingoes are the only native animals that people can keep as pets. This is not the case across the nation, and it is still illegal to keep a pet dingo in some places.

People who do keep pet dingoes find that they are not as easy to train as dogs. Pet dingoes tend to form a single bond with one human and remain wary of everyone else. They should not be kept in households with children or other pets.

# WHERE TO SEE DINGOES

Caretaker feeding dingoes in a wildlife park

Most zoos and wildlife parks in Australia keep dingoes. Some places allow visitors to pat their dingoes under supervision.

Fraser Island is famous for its dingo population. Campers will not only see dingoes, but may have to protect themselves, their food and their children from wild dingoes that are curious, fearless and smart.

# DINGOES VERSUS TASMANIAN TIGERS

Tasmanian tiger

Dingoes and Tasmanian tigers, or thylacines, both lived on the mainland of Australia up until a few thousand years ago. They competed for the same sort of food and dingoes may have hunted and killed thylacines. There are no dingoes in Tasmania, so they were never a threat to the thylacines there.

# THE FUTURE OF DINGOES

Pure-bred dingoes are not common. Because dingoes and domestic dogs breed together, many dingo populations are cross-bred. As people move further into dingo territories, taking their domestic dogs with them, the pure-bred dingo will become rarer.

Cross-bred dingoes can be in feral dog packs that attack livestock and wildlife.

# SHOOTING DINGOES

Dingoes are not considered native animals in all parts of Australia. Some places treat them as nuisance wild dogs or as pests. This means they can be killed by shooting or baiting.

The inter-breeding of dingoes with feral dogs makes it very difficult to tell whether animals that are attacking livestock are dingoes or not. Some cross-bred dogs look very much like pure-bred dingoes.

# OLD DINGO TALES

## 1699

"... my men saw two or three beasts like hungry wolves, lean like so many skeletons, being nothing but skin and bones ..."

William Dampier, A Voyage To New-Holland, &c. In the Year 1699. (Writing about the coast of Western Australia.)

A
VOYAGE
TO
NEW-HOLLAND, &c.
In the YEAR 1699.

Wherein are deſcribed,
The *Canary*-Iſlands, the Iſles of *Mayo* and St. *Jago*. The Bay of *All-Saints*, with the Forts and Town of *Bahia* in *Brazil*. Cape *Salvadore*. The Winds on the *Braſilian* Coaſt. *Abrohlo* Shoals. A Table of all the *Variations* obſerv'd in this Voyage. Occurrences near the Cape of *Good-Hope*. The Courſe to *New-Holland*. *Shark's* Bay. The Iſles and Coaſt, *&c.* of *New-Holland*.
Their Inhabitants, Manners, Cuſtoms, Trade, *&c.* Their Harbours, Soil, Beaſts, Birds, Fiſh, *&c.* Trees, Plants, Fruits, *&c.*

Illuſtrated with ſeveral MAPS and DRAUGHTS: Alſo divers Birds, Fiſhes and Plants not found in this Part of the World, Curiouſly Ingraven on Copper-Plates.

By Captain WILLIAM DAMPIER.

*The* THIRD EDITION.

*LONDON*,
Printed for JAMES *and* JOHN KNAPTON, at the *Crown* in St. *Paul's* Church-Yard. MDCCXXIX.

## 1789

"The only domestic animal they have is the dog, which in their language is called dingo ... One of them is now in the possession of the Governor, and tolerably well reconciled to his new master."

Watkin Tench, Narrative of the Expedition to Botany Bay, 1789. (Writing about the Aboriginal people near Sydney.)

## 1789

"DOG OF NEW SOUTH WALES... It has much of the manners of the dog, but is of a very savage nature, and not likely to change in this particular."

The Voyage of Governor Phillip to Botany Bay, 1789.

## 1825

"Kangaroo, large and small opossum, flying squirrels, and wild dogs, were seen."

Major Lockyer, Sydney Gazette, 1825. (Writing after seeing the Brisbane River for the first time.)

# SORTING ANIMALS INTO GROUPS

Biologists divide all living things around the world into groups. They call this process classification.

Here are the basic groups that describe all animals with backbones:

### AMPHIBIANS

Examples include frogs and salamanders. Amphibians start life in water but later grow lungs so they can breathe air on land.

### MAMMALS

Examples include dingoes and possums. Mammals are warm-blooded, have fur and feed their young on milk.

### FISH

Examples include sharks and goldfish.

### BIRDS

Examples include emus and penguins. Birds are the only animals with feathers.

### REPTILES

Examples include lizards and snakes. Reptiles are cold-blooded and are covered in scales.

Mammals are further divided into three main groups:

### MONOTREME MAMMALS

Examples include echidnas and platypuses. Monotreme mammals lay eggs.

### MARSUPIAL MAMMALS

Examples include kangaroos and koalas. Marsupial mammals produce tiny, underdeveloped babies that continue to grow inside their parent's pouch.

### PLACENTAL MAMMALS

Examples include whales and humans. Placental mammals have or once had fur, and they grow their babies inside their bodies.

Humans have a scientific name and a position in the classification of animals. We are called *Homo sapiens*. These Latin words mean 'smart person'.

# WILD DOGS OF THE WORLD

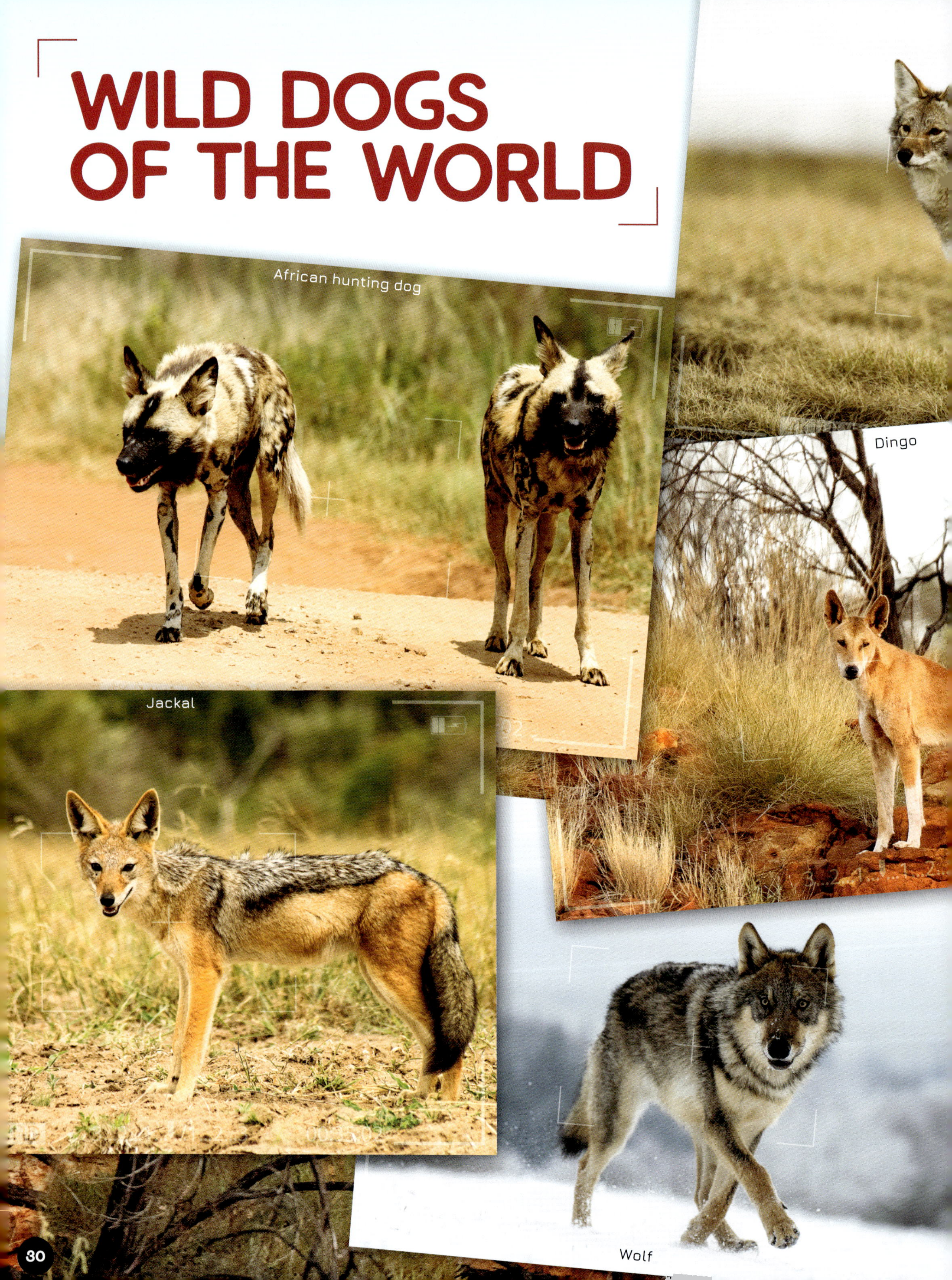

African hunting dog

Dingo

Jackal

Wolf

Coyote

# GLOSSARY

**canis** group that includes domestic, wild and native dogs

**carnivore** animal that eats mainly meat

**habitat** normal place in the wild where an animal lives

**millennia** thousands of years

**placental animal** animal whose young develop inside the mother's body, attached to her bloodstream through a placenta

**prey** animal that another animal eats

**semi-arid** having a rainfall level which is low, but more than in a desert region

**territory** part of a habitat claimed and defended by one animal or a small group

# INDEX